D0902567

Secrets, statistics, and little-known facts about basketball

Bruce Adelson

illustrations by Harry Pulver Jr.

Lerner Publications Company • Minneapolis

For Sharon Craig, Vicki Fagliarone, Laurie Goss, Sally Keyes, Jan McConnel, and Lorraine Nasiatka—second grade teachers at Zachary Taylor Elementary School in Arlington, Virginia. Your dedication, collegiality, and professionalism will inspire me for years to come. Thank you.

—B.A.

Thank you to Wayne Patterson and the library staff of the Naismith Memorial Basketball Hall of Fame in Springfield, Massachusetts, for their help in researching this book. The assistance of Kevin Coonce, Anna Nelson, Nick O'Hora, Erin Statler, and Tiffany Volkman of Joan Yocum's fifth grade language arts class at Zachary Taylor Elementary School is gratefully acknowledged. Your exuberance and helpful review of this book contributed to its completion. Thanks as well to Joan Yocum, whose enthusiasm for our writing project will always be appreciated.

—B.A.

Illustrations by Harry Pulver Jr.
Book design and electronic prepress: Steve Foley, Mike Kohn, Sean Todd

Copyright © 1998 Bruce Adelson

Second printing 1999 contains updated information

All rights reserved. International copyright secured. No part of this book may be reproduced or transmitted in any form or by any means, electronic or mechanical, including photocopying and recording, or by any information storage or retrieval system, without permission in writing from Lerner Publications Company, except for the inclusion of brief quotations in an acknowledged review.

Website address: www.lernerbooks.com

Library of Congress Cataloging-in-Publication Data

Adelson, Bruce.
    Slam dunk trivia / by Bruce Adelson ; illustrations by Harry Pulver, Jr.
      p. cm.
    Includes bibliographical references and index.
    Summary: Presents facts and figures about the game of basketball—past and present, especially professional play in the NBA.
      ISBN 0-8225-3313-8 (hardcover : alk. paper). — ISBN 0-8225-9804-3 (paperback : alk. paper)
      1. Basketball—Miscellanea—Juvenile literature. 2. Basketball—Records—Juvenile literature. [1. Basketball—Miscellanea.] I. Pulver, Harry, ill. II. Title.
GV885.1.A34   1998
796.323—dc21   97–50006

Manufactured in the United States of America
2 3 4 5 6 7 - JR - 04 03 02 01 00 99

Contents

Chapter 1

The Game of Basketball

Dr. James Naismith, a teacher at a school in Springfield, Massachusetts, invented basketball in 1891 as a new game for his students to play. In the beginning, the idea was to toss and not slam the ball—which at first was a soccer ball—into one of two peach baskets. The baskets were nailed to the walls at opposite ends of the court.

James Naismith fine-tunes the game later known as basketball.

Naismith (right center) poses with the first basketball team, at the YMCA Training School in Springfield.

Did You Know?

When James Naismith invented basketball in 1891, he did not have a name for his new sport. Frank Mahan, a player on the first basketball team, suggested it be called Naismith Ball in honor of the game's creator. After thinking about it, Naismith decided he did not like Frank's idea. Instead, he had his own inspiration for a name. "We have a basket and a ball and it seems to me that would be a good name for it," said Naismith. Naismith's game, "basket ball," was spelled with two words until 1921.

Players brought the peach basket outdoors for a game in 1892.

Besides peach baskets, Naismith's students also played games with garbage cans as basketball hoops. Besides having solid sides and no nets, they also had bottoms, so when balls were tossed into the baskets, they stayed inside. For a shot to score, the ball had to go into the basket and not come back out. After each score, the game stopped. The referee would take a ladder, climb up to the basket, and remove the ball. He then carried the ball to center court where he started play with a jump ball for one player from each team. They repeated this procedure each time a score was made.

Did You Know?

When Dr. Naismith invented basketball, he was not thinking of using peach baskets or garbage cans. Instead, he first considered using boxes for basketball hoops. He asked his school custodian, Pop Stebbins, to find two boxes for his new game. Pop was unable to find two solid boxes but he did discover two good peach baskets that he gave to Dr. Naismith, who used them for his game. Imagine what basketball would have been called if Pop Stebbins had found the boxes? Instead of basketball, Dr. Naismith's invention might have been named Box Ball!

The first basketball game was played at a YMCA in Springfield, Massachusetts, on December 21, 1891. No one was allowed to watch the teams play. The first public game was played four months later, on March 4, 1892, with students and teachers at Dr. Naismith's school playing against each other. The students won the game, 5-1, in front of a crowd of 500 people. (Each basket only scored one point. A few years later the scoring rules would change, and baskets would earn three points.) Backboards were not used until 1893. Eventually, backboards were added to prevent fan interference. Some fans sitting or standing in the row of seats above the basket would block shots from the opposing team or guide shots from their team into their basket. In 1895, backboards were wire. But some teams bent the wire backboards to create grooves, making it easier for their team to shoot the ball into the basket below the curved backboard. Wood backboards were used beginning in 1904. Two years later, glass backboards were invented. In 1912 the bottoms of the baskets were opened to speed up the game. The jump ball at center court after each score stayed in place until 1937, however. Transparent fiberglass backboards, similar to the ones in the National Basketball Association, were first used in 1946.

Did You Know?

In 1979 Darryl Dawkins of the Philadelphia 76ers smashed two backboards within a month. Darryl named the first smashup job the "Chocolate-Thunder-Flying, Robinzine-Crying, Teeth-Shaking, Glass-Breaking, Rump-Roasting, Bun-Toasting, Wham-Bam, Glass-Breaker-I-Am Jam."

Fans crowd around an early basketball game. The young players wore light or dark pants to distinguish the two teams. The backboard they used was made of wire mesh.

Trivia Teaser #1

Why are basketball players also called "cagers?"

Absolutely no physical contact between the players was allowed in the first basketball games. One of Dr. Naismith's original rules said that if one player fouled another player intentionally, he would be removed from the game and would not be allowed to return. Back then that rule could present a real problem, because teams could not substitute for players who had to leave the game. Player substitutions were not permitted until 1894. If the referee thought that a player was being too rough or "ungentlemanly," he was prevented from playing for the rest of the season.

The earliest teams did not have a set number of players. Five-person teams did not become official until 1895. Even after that, some colleges still used seven-person teams. For uniforms, players wore knicker-type pants that came down to just below the knee. The players also wore high stockings. Their shirts were sleeveless and looked very much like those worn by modern-day basketball players.

Did You Know?

The first college basketball game was played on January 16, 1896. The University of Chicago defeated the University of Iowa, 15–12. Neither team made any substitutions. The first professional basketball game was played later that year, on November 7, 1896, in Trenton, New Jersey. The Trenton Basket Ball team beat the Brooklyn YMCA 16–1. After the game, the players were paid $15 each. The year 1896 was also when the scoring rules again changed, this time to a system that remained in place for good. Field goal points changed from three to two and foul shots counted for one point instead of three.

The University of Kansas's first varsity basketball team played during the 1898–99 season. Naismith (upper right) was the team's coach.

Youngsters enjoy a game of basketball in about 1915, before unlimited dribbling was allowed.

In the early years of basketball, players were not allowed to dribble the ball as much as they wanted. Players could only dribble a certain number of times. From 1901 to 1908, the player dribbling the basketball was not even allowed to shoot the ball. In 1927 the Basketball Rules Committee passed a rule that said players could only dribble the ball once. Eventually, this changed, and players can dribble the basketball an unlimited number of times.

Soccer balls were used in basketball games until 1894. That year, the Overman Wheel Company of Chicopee Falls, Massachusetts, made the first basketballs. While the new sport now had its own ball, no one was sure what the color of the basketballs should be.

There was no rule that required all teams to use balls of the same color so their colors changed over the years. In

1934, college basketballs were black. By the next year, balls of many colors were used, including black and orange. In 1939, some teams used white basketballs.

By the 1950s, a decision still had not been made about the color of basketballs. In 1957, tan balls had to be used but yellow basketballs were also permitted in games if both teams agreed. College basketball officials then did a study to choose the best color for their basketballs. Tests were done to see which color would be the best for fans, players, and referees to see. Everyone picked orange basketballs. People thought that orange basketballs would be the easiest for everyone to follow during games.

Orange became the official color of basketballs for the 1960 season. Yellow balls could not be used in games anymore. Tan basketballs could still be used only because teams had so many of them.

Trivia Teaser #2

I play center for a team in the Western Conference of the National Basketball Association. I am originally from Nigeria. Translated into English, my name means "Always Being on Top." In my 13-year career, I have scored 23,842 points. Only 14 players in NBA history have scored more points than I have. In 1994 and 1995, my team won the NBA Championship. Who am I?

Dunking a basketball is one of the most exciting plays you will see in a basketball game. Although slam dunks are a regular part of modern basketball, dunking has not always been permitted. When Dr. Naismith first invented basketball, there was no rule against dunking—probably because he never imagined it was possible. In basketball's early years, players did not even jump when shooting. They shot the ball with two hands, without jumping up in the air. Shooting the ball with two hands without jumping is called a set shot.

Early basketball players were also typically much shorter than players in the 1990s. In 1937, the average height of players in the National Basketball League—a professional basketball league before the National Basketball Association (NBA) was formed in 1946—was only 6 feet 1 inch. Only six players were over 6 feet 5 inches. Basketball players over 7 feet tall were extremely unusual. In contrast, NBA players in 1997 averaged 6 feet 8 inches.

Early set shot

By the 1940s, basketball was changing. Players were taller, and they also began to discover new ways of shooting a basketball. They began using the jump shot, leaping into the air and shooting. In 1940, Kenny Sailors played basketball for the University of Wyoming. He is thought to be the first player to use a jump shot in college basketball.

George Mikan (left) jumped so high that officials tried raising the baskets. Jumping Joe Fulks (right, #10) rose up to the basket as well as any of his rivals.

George Mikan played center for the Minneapolis Lakers. At 6-foot-10, he was the first dominant "big man" in basketball history. He was such a good player that the National Basketball League passed a rule raising the height of the basket from 10 feet to 12 feet to reduce the advantage Mikan had over other players. Because Mikan was still able to shoot over everyone else, and because the other players were uncomfortable with the new, taller basket, this change lasted for only one game.

Jumping Joe Fulks also played professional basketball in the 1940s. He became famous for using the jump shot and the one-handed shot in the NBA. On February 10, 1949, Jumping Joe became the first NBA player to score 60 points in one game. George Mikan and Joe Fulks are members of basketball's Hall of Fame.

Although basketball players in the 1940s were taller and were jumping more than in the early years of basketball, they still did not dunk in games. Many players had the ability to dunk a basketball, but dunking during a game was considered impolite. People felt that dunking against another player would embarrass him. Jim Pollard, nicknamed The Kangaroo Kid because of his jumping ability, played basketball in the 1940s and 1950s. He would dunk the basketball during practices—taking off into the air from the foul line and jamming the ball through the hoop—to entertain his teammates. But he did not dunk in games.

Did You Know?

In a typical NBA game, the average player runs the equivalent of 2.4 miles.

Did You Know?

In 1986, Spud Webb played in the NBA for the Atlanta Hawks. Although he was only 5 feet 7 inches tall, he still won the Slam Dunk Contest at the All-Star Game, defeating players who were much taller and bigger than he was. Although he was not tall, he could jump very high. Webb could jump 42 inches into the air.

In 1945 Bob Kurland, who played college basketball for Oklahoma A&M, became the first player to dunk the ball regularly. Back then, dunking had another name. A newspaper called it a "duffer shot." Eventually more players started to dunk the ball in college games until dunking was banned in 1967. Dunking was not allowed again in college basketball until 1976.

Bob Kurland *Connie Hawkins*

Dunking did not become popular in the NBA until the 1960s. Connie "The Hawk" Hawkins, who played seven years in the NBA in the 1960s and 1970s, was famous for all kinds of fancy shots and dunks. He is credited with making the dunk popular in NBA games. From Connie Hawkins, other players, such as Julius "Dr. J" Erving, learned about different kinds of shots. Dr. Jr., who played for the Philadelphia 76ers in the 1970s and 1980s, entertained the crowds with his high-flying dunks. Erving could jump from the foul line, 15 feet from the basket, and slam dunk the ball. With his tremendous leaping ability, he could reach as high as 12 feet off the floor. Both the Hawk and Dr. J. are members of basketball's Hall of Fame. Their style of play influenced Michael Jordan and other basketball stars of the 1990s.

Chapter Two

African Americans in Basketball

In the early days of basketball, African Americans played the new sport mainly in local YMCAs and several colleges. Then, blacks who wanted to play basketball were forced to play mainly on teams with only other black players. In the late 1890s and the early 1900s, most teams were not integrated. Samuel Ransom, who played for Beloit College in

Samuel Ransom, second row, far right, and his Beloit College teammates

Did You Know?

In 1942, the Chicago Studebakers played in the National Basketball League. Although they played only one season, the Studebakers are today thought to be one of the first integrated teams in professional major league sports. Six African Americans played for Chicago with several white players.

Wisconsin from 1904 to 1908, is thought to be the first African American to integrate a previously all-white basketball team. Despite the integration of several college teams, professional basketball was not ready to integrate.

In the 1920s, the New York Renaissance and the Harlem Globetrotters were formed. These professional basketball teams, with only African American players, became two of the most famous basketball organizations in history. The Renaissance, known as the Rens, were named after the Renaissance Casino Ballroom, where they played their home games. The team toured the country, playing against other professional basketball teams.

Back then, many places throughout the United States discriminated against African Americans by preventing them from staying in the same hotels and eating in the same restaurants as white people. In some places, Renaissance players were insulted, taunted, and even spat at by people just because they did not like their skin color. Often, the Rens were not allowed to stay in any hotels in the towns where they played. Sometimes, the Rens would drive 200 miles to another city to play a game, then drive home again,

Clarence Jenkins, a member of the original Renaissance team

sleep, and do the same thing again the next day. This way they avoided spending the night in other cities where they weren't allowed in the hotels. Other times the players slept and ate aboard their custom-made $10,000 team bus. During most seasons, they played games almost every night of the week.

From 1932 to 1936, the Rens won 473 games and lost only 49. At one point, they won 88 games in a row. In 1939 the Rens won 112 of the 119 games they played. They also defeated the Oshkosh All-Stars, the champions of the National Basketball League, which did not allow African American players. From 1922 until they went out of business in 1949, the Rens won 2,588 games and lost just 529. In 1963, the entire team became members of basketball's Hall of Fame.

The Harlem Globetrotters were formed in 1927. The Globetrotters and the Rens developed a rivalry. In 1940 the Globetrotters defeated the Renaissance 37–36 to become the champions of black professional basketball. Over the years, the Globetrotters became famous. They have played basketball all over the world. Still playing today, the Harlem Globetrotters are the oldest professional African American sports team in United States history.

The original Globetrotters pose with manager Abe Saperstein (left).

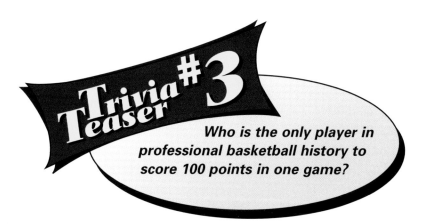

Trivia Teaser #3

Who is the only player in professional basketball history to score 100 points in one game?

Chuck Cooper

In the 1930s and 1940s, several African Americans played basketball for otherwise all-white college teams. In 1946 the University of Tennessee and the University of Miami refused to play a game against Duquesne University of Pittsburgh because one of Duquesne's players was Chuck Cooper, an African American. Only four years later, Chuck Cooper would make history as the first black man to sign a contract to play for a team in the NBA.

Though blacks and whites played together on college teams, this was not true in professional basketball until 1950. That year, three players became the first African Americans to play in the NBA. Chuck Cooper was drafted by the Boston Celtics, Earl Lloyd by the Washington Capitols and Nat "Sweetwater" Clifton by the New York Knickerbockers. Earl Lloyd became the first of the trio to play in an NBA game on October 31, 1950—only 24 hours before Chuck Cooper played in a game for Boston. Nat Clifton played in his first NBA game on November 4, 1950.

Not everyone was ready to accept African Americans in the NBA. Some people called out racial insults to these players during games. When the teams with African American players had exhibition games in the South, where laws still prevented blacks and whites from playing sports or eating together, Earl Lloyd, Nat Clifton, and Chuck Cooper were often left at home.

These three men opened the door for other African American players to enter the NBA. It took about ten more years before black players played in large numbers in the NBA. In the late 1950s, Bill Russell, Elgin Baylor, Hal Greer, and Sam Jones all began their NBA careers.

Sam Jones

These four famous African American athletes helped make it easier for black players to enter the league in greater numbers. Many more African American athletes played in the NBA in the 1960s. By the 1990s over 80 percent of the players in the NBA were African American.

Which player has scored more points than anyone else in the history of the National Basketball Association?

A. Michael Jordan

B. Wilt Chamberlain

C. Kareem Abdul-Jabbar

D. Karl Malone

Who is the shortest player in NBA history?

A: **C. Kareem Abdul-Jabbar** scored 38,387 points in his 20-year NBA career, which began with the 1969–70 season and ended in 1989. He played center for the Milwaukee Bucks and Los Angeles Lakers. At 7-foot-2, Abdul-Jabbar led the Lakers to five NBA championship titles in the 1980s. He also is the all-time NBA leader in most field goals made, most field goals attempted, and most games played. He won the Most Valuable Player award six times. Abdul-Jabbar is a member of the Basketball Hall of Fame.

Did You Know?

Wilt Chamberlain and Bill Russell are probably the two best rebounders in NBA history. They also played against each other often in the 1960s. In his career, Wilt had 23,924 rebounds, making him number 1 on the all-time list. Bill had 21,620, making him number 2 on the list. The number-3 player, Kareem Abdul-Jabbar, had almost 4,000 fewer rebounds (17,440) although he played more years in the NBA than Wilt or Bill did. Wilt Chamberlain holds the record for most rebounds in one game with 55. Bill is second with 51.

Bill Russell

Wilt Chamberlain

Trivia Teaser #5

Why is there a 24-second clock in National Basketball Association games?

Chapter Three

Women and Basketball

Did You Know?

Senda Berenson Abbott is known as the Mother of Women's Basketball. The physical education director at Smith College in Massachusetts in the 1890s, she learned about Dr. Naismith's basketball invention by reading about it in a magazine. Berenson then adapted the new sport for women to play.

The first women's game took place in March 1892 in Springfield, Massachusetts, at the same YMCA where Dr. Naismith had invented the sport. About one year later, Senda Berenson began teaching basketball to students at Smith College. The women's game quickly spread to other colleges and schools.

Many people were concerned that basketball was too difficult for women to play. They felt that women were not strong enough to play such a physically demanding sport. To reduce the running women would have to do, Berenson divided the basketball court into three equal sections. Players had to stay in their assigned sections. This way, women players did not have to run up and down the court.

Berenson's team at Smith College (left) poses for a group photo. The numbers they wear indicate the graduating class of 1895. Another group of women (above) play an outdoor game.

Berenson eventually took responsibility for publishing official rules for women's basketball. As the game spread, however, other promoters of the sport set up the game differently. Some basketball courts had as many as 11 squares, with up to 21 women playing basketball in each. Women's basketball courts were also kept smaller than men's courts.

Trivia Teaser #6

In high school, I once scored 105 points in one game. I went to college at the University of Southern California. I hold almost every record at my school. I was a four-time All-American. I also won an Olympic gold medal with the U. S. women's basketball team in 1984. Many people believe I am the greatest women's basketball player of all time. WHO AM I?

Early women's games were very different from modern women's basketball in other ways. At first, dribbling was not allowed. Players were not permitted to guard other players on the court. Yelling or talking during games was prohibited. If a player aimed the ball at the hoop and did not shoot, this was considered a foul.

Things started to change in the twentieth century. Women players were allowed to dribble by 1903, but the number of times they could dribble the ball was limited. Women were not given the unlimited dribble until 1966. Guarding of other players was permitted in 1932. The bottoms of the basketball hoops (baskets) were opened in 1917, five years after they were opened for men's games.

During the first half of the century, women's uniforms often included bloomers.

When women first started playing basketball, coaching from the sidelines was considered a foul. Teammates were not even allowed to speak to one another. This changed in 1916. Players then were only permitted to speak quietly. Team coaches were not allowed to coach or talk to their players during timeouts or between quarters until the 1950s.

Over the years, women began to play basketball according to almost the same rules as men. The three-section court became a two-section court in 1938. By the end of the 1940s, defensive guarding was allowed. In the 1950s, the rules were changed to allow the coaching of players at intermissions or time-outs. In 1966 the unlimited dribble was allowed in women's basketball. In 1971 an experimental rule permitting women to play all five players on a full court became official. By this time, most basketball rules were the same or similar for men and women.

Beginning in the 1970s, the Association for Intercollegiate Athletics for Women sponsored the first official national championships for women's college basketball.

Did You Know?

The Baskin High School Lady Rams hold the record for the longest winning streak of all-time, for any high school, college, or professional women's or men's team. From 1947 to 1953, this Louisiana high school basketball team won an incredible 218 straight games.

Players scramble for control of the ball in a game at which the only spectators are female schoolmates and nuns.

Since 1982, the National Collegiate Athletic Association (NCAA) has held national championships. Games were televised, and thousands of fans packed the stands.

On December 19, 1978, more than 7,800 people watched the official opening of the Women's Professional

Basketball League, the first pro league for women. Enthusiasm was high, but the league only lasted for four seasons before financial problems caused it to fold. In the 1980s, many talented women went overseas to play professional basketball.

Trivia Teaser #7

A smooth, talented member of UCLA's women's basketball team from 1975 to 1978, this player joined the U. S. women's team for the 1976 Olympics. In 1979 she became the first woman to sign with an NBA team. Although she never played in an NBA game, this outstanding athlete later became the first woman inducted into the Basketball Hall of Fame. **WHO IS SHE?**

In 1976, Lusia Harris scored the first basket in the history of women's Olympic basketball. As a three-time All-American college player at Delta State in Mississippi, Harris scored 2,981 points (25.9 points per game average) and collected 1,662 rebounds (14.4 rebounds per game). The Lady Statesman, her college team, won 109 of the 115 games they played with Harris.

Nancy Lieberman, who played basketball at Old Dominion University in Virginia, was a three-time All-American college player. In 1986, she became the first woman to play in a men's professional league, the United States Basketball League. She also played for the Dallas Diamonds in the Women's Professional Basketball League. Lusia Harris and Nancy Lieberman are both members of basketball's Hall of Fame.

Nancy Lieberman goes up for a shot.

Did You Know?

On December 21, 1984, Georgeann Wells, the 6 foot 7 inch center for West Virginia University women's basketball team, became the first woman to dunk a basketball during a regular game. She did it in the second half against Charleston College. West Virginia won the game 110–82.

Did you Know?

Dee Kantner and Violet Palmer made history in 1997 when they became NBA referees. They are the first women ever to referee regular season games for a major U.S. pro sports league.

The following are descriptions of four pro players. Try to match the descriptions to each of these women: *Cynthia Cooper, Teresa Edwards, Lisa Leslie, Sylvia Crawley.*

A. I am 6 foot 5 and I play for the ABL's Colorado Xplosion. I won the slam dunk contest at the 1998 ABL All-Star Game, when I hit a blindfolded one-handed slam for a perfect score of 50.

B. I play forward for the WNBA's Los Angeles Sparks. In 1997 I was named to the All-WNBA first team. I led the league in rebounds per game (9.3) and was second in blocked shots per game (2.16). In 1996 I won an Olympic gold medal playing with the U.S. women's team.

C. I play guard for the Houston Comets of the WNBA. I was named the league's Most Valuable Player in 1997. I led the WNBA in scoring, averaging 22.2 points per game. That year I also set a WNBA record by scoring 44 points in a game against the Sacramento Monarchs.

D. I play guard and forward for the ABL's Atlanta Glory. I am also the team's coach. In 1997 I scored 46 points in a game against the Seattle Reign. I am the only athlete to have played on four U.S. Olympic basketball teams.

A: *Cynthia Cooper-C. Teresa Edwards-D. Lisa Leslie-B. Sylvia Crawley-A.*

Never had a U.S. women's national team received as much recognition as the gold-medal winners of the 1996 Olympics. The U.S. team played on a worldwide tour preceding the Olympic Games in August 1996, winning 60 games and losing none. Many of the members of the 1996 U.S. women's team went on to play for one of two pro leagues for women. The American Basketball League (ABL) played its first season the winter of 1995–96. The Women's National Basketball Association (WNBA) played its first season the following summer. Both leagues feature many of the world's top female players.

Players on the U. S. women's team celebrate winning the gold at the 1996 Olympics in Atlanta, Georgia.

Chapter Four

Statistics

Did You Know?

The highest scoring game in National Basketball Association history took place on December 13, 1983. The Detroit Pistons played the Nuggets in Denver. Five players, Isaiah Thomas (47), Kelly Tripucka (35), and John Long (41) for Detroit and Alex English (47) and Kiki Vandeweghe (51) for Denver scored more than 30 points apiece. The teams played three overtime periods. The final score was Detroit, 186, and Denver, 184. The game lasted more than 3 hours.

Michael Jordan

Statistics are kept for each NBA game. NBA stats involve averages and percentages and are easy to figure out. You can compare players' scoring averages, free throw percentages, and field goal percentages.

Michael Jordan retired in 1999 with the highest scoring average in NBA history. In his 13-year career, he scored 29,277 points. This includes 6,798 free throws (awarded after a foul) and 10,962 field goals (regular shots). Jordan played in 930 games during those 13 years. To calculate his scoring average, we figure out the average number of points he scored per game. Divide points by games played.

$$29,277 \div 930 = 31.480$$

Round this number up to 31.5 This is the average number of points Michael Jordan scored in each game during his 13-year NBA career.

Trivia Teaser #8

I play for the Utah Jazz. My nickname is The Mailman. In 12 years in the NBA, I have scored 26,777 points. Only 5 players in National Basketball Association history have scored more points than I have. WHO AM I?

Did You Know?

Besides having the highest scoring average in NBA history, Michael Jordan also holds the NBA record for most points in a playoff game. He scored 63 points against the Boston Celtics on April 21, 1986. Michael also led the NBA in scoring for ten seasons, 1987 through 1993 and 1998. No other player in NBA history has led the league in scoring as often as Michael Jordan has.

Let's figure out David Robinson's scoring average. Take his points (15,470) and divide by the number of games he has played (611).

$$15{,}470 \div 611 = 25.3$$

David Robinson's 25.3 scoring average, or points per game average, is the 9th best in NBA history.

David Robinson   *Shaquille O'Neal*

Percentages are used to figure out how accurately a player shoots. Field goal percentages measure the number of times a player makes a shot, also called a field goal, compared to the number of times he shoots.

From 1992 to 1997, Shaquille O'Neal attempted 6,513 field goals. Out of these shots, he scored 3,760 times and missed 2,753 times. To figure out Shaq's field goal percentage, we divide.

$$3{,}760 \div 6{,}513 = .5773$$

Round this to .577. Move the decimal point two places to the right. O'Neal has made 57.7 percent of his shots.

The all-time NBA field goal percentage leader is Artis Gilmore, who played in the NBA in the 1970s and 1980s. Out of 9,570 field goals Gilmore attempted, he made 5,732.

$$5,732 \div 9,570 = .5989$$

Round this number to .599, move the decimal point, and you get 59.9. His average is 59.9 percent.

Free throw percentage measures how accurately players shoot foul shots. Mark Price has the best free throw percentage in NBA history. To get Mark's percentage, take the number of free throws he has made (2,115) and divide by the number he has attempted (2,332).

$$2,115 \div 2,332 = .9069$$

Round this number to .907 and move the decimal point two places to the right. Mark's free throw percentage is 90.7 percent. He has made 90.7 percent, or more than 9 out of 10, of the foul shots he has taken.

Trivia Teaser #9

I play guard for the Orlando Magic. In 1994, my second NBA season, I averaged 20.9 points per game and I was selected to the NBA All-Star team. My nickname is Penny.
WHO AM I?

Q: *Which NBA player holds the all-time record for best three-point field goal percentage?*

A. Michael Jordan

B. Reggie Miller

C. Clyde Drexler

D. Steve Kerr

A: ***Steve Kerr.*** Kerr, who plays for the Chicago Bulls, attempted 1,221 three-point shots in 10 NBA seasons. He made 577 of them.

$$577 \div 1{,}221 = .4726$$

His three-point field goal percentage is .473 or about 47 percent. Kerr has made almost half of the three-point shots he has taken.

Chapter Five

Basketball's Best Players

Over the years, the statistics of every NBA player have been recorded. Here is a collection of the statistics on some of basketball's greatest players. They are divided into five different categories that will tell you the top five players with the most career points, the best scoring averages, the best field goal percentages, the best free throw percentages, and the most rebounds in NBA history. The stats of some key players of the '90s are also shown, so you can see how your favorites match up against basketball's all-time best players.

Most Points

Kareem Abdul–Jabbar	38,387
Wilt Chamberlain	31,419
Moses Malone	27,409
Elvin Hayes	27,313
Oscar Robertson	26,710

Wilt Chamberlain

Players of the '90s

Michael Jordan	29,277
Karl Malone	27,782
Hakeem Olajuwon	24,422
Robert Parish	23,334
Charles Barkley	22,792

Many NBA players have very colorful nicknames. See how many players you can
match with their nicknames. Some of them
are playing in the NBA. Others are former players who are in basketball's Hall of Fame. Be careful! Some
players have more than one nickname.

Players:	Nicknames:
George Gervin	The Round Mound of Rebound
Alonzo Mourning	The Big O
Wilt Chamberlain	The Dream
Oscar Robertson	The Human Highlight Film
David Robinson	'Nique
Charles Barkley	'Zo
Hakeem Olajuwon	Wilt the Stilt
Dominique Wilkins	Dollar Bill
Elvin Hayes	Hondo
Michael Jordan	The Big E
John Havlicek	Air
David Thompson	Sir Charles
Bill Bradley	The Skywalker
	The Iceman
	The Admiral

A: *Charles Barkley has two nicknames: The Round Mound of Rebound and Sir Charles. Oscar Robertson is The Big O. Hakeem Olajuwon is The Dream. Dominique Wilkins is known as 'Nique and The Human Highlight Film. Alonzo Mourning is called 'Zo. David Robinson is The Admiral. Wilt Chamberlain is Wilt the Stilt. Bill Bradley is Dollar Bill. John Havlicek is Hondo. Elvin Hayes is The Big E. Michael Jordan is Air. David Thompson is The Skywalker. George Gervin is The Iceman.*

Best Free Throw Percentage

Mark Price	.907
Rick Barry	.900
Calvin Murphy	.892
Scott Skiles	.889
Larry Bird	.886

Players of the '90s

Reggie Miller	.877
Ricky Pierce	.876
Jeff Malone	.871
Michael Jordan	.840
John Stockton	.823

Mark Price

Best Scoring Average

Michael Jordan	31.6
Wilt Chamberlain	30.1
Elgin Baylor	27.4
Jerry West	27.0
Bob Petit	26.4

Players of the '90s

Karl Malone	26.1
David Robinson	25.3
Hakeem Olajuwon	24.1
Clyde Drexler	20.5
Anfernee Hardaway	19.6

Reggie Miller

Bob Cousy

Did You Know?

Many players can dribble the basketball between their legs and behind their backs. However, when Bob Cousy played for the Boston Celtics in the 1950s, almost no one did this—except Cousy. He was one of the first NBA players to use fancy plays, or "razzle dazzle," in his game. He was nicknamed The Houdini of the Hardwood because he fooled so many players with his fancy plays, like Houdini fooled people with magic tricks. Bob Cousy is a member of basketball's Hall of Fame.

Trivia Teaser #10

The Chicago Bulls won the 1996 NBA Championship after winning 72 games in the regular season, an NBA record. Which NBA team has won more games and more championships than any other?

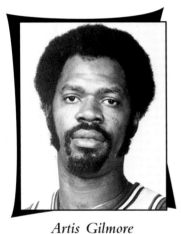

Artis Gilmore

David Robinson

Best Field Goal Percentage

Artis Gilmore	.599
Mark West	.585
Shaquille O'Neal	.579
Steve Johnson	.572
Darryl Dawkins	.572

Players of the '90s

David Robinson	.526
Dikembe Mutombo	.524
Patrick Ewing	.513
Michael Jordan	.506
Scottie Pippen	.484

Most Rebounds

Wilt Chamberlain	23,924
Bill Russell	21,620
Kareem Abdul-Jabbar	17,440
Elvin Hayes	16,279
Moses Malone	16,212

Players of the '90s

Hakeem Olajuwon	12,199
Charles Barkley	11,821
Karl Malone	11,376
Patrick Ewing	9,778
Dikembe Mutombo	6,672

Elvin Hayes

Charles Barkley

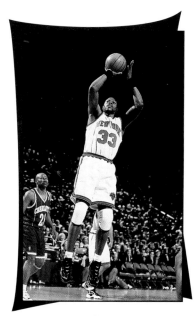

Patrick Ewing

Trivia Teaser Answers

#1 *Answer: Until the 1920s, floor to ceiling nets or wire cages surrounded many basketball courts to keep the balls from going out of bounds.* Players often ran into the cages during games. After games, players discovered that they were covered with all kinds of bruises from hitting the wire. *Since early games were played inside these cages, the players were also called cagers.*

#2

Answer: Hakeem Olajuwon. He plays for the Houston Rockets. Hakeem is also the only player in NBA history to win the NBA Most Valuable Player Award, Defensive Player of the Year Award, and Most Valuable Player Award for the NBA Finals in the same year. He did it in 1994, when Houston won its first championship by defeating the New York Knickerbockers. Hakeem is also the all-time NBA leader in career blocked shots. He had 3,459 through the 1997-98 season.

Hakeem Olajuwon

#3

Answer: Wilt Chamberlain. On March 2, 1962, Chamberlain of the Philadelphia Warriors scored 100 points against the New York Knickerbockers. When the first quarter of that game had ended, Chamberlain had already scored 23 points. By the end of the third quarter, he had 69 points. Chamberlain scored on 36 of the 63 shots he took in the game. He also made 28 free throws. Philadelphia won the game 169-147. That year, 1962, was a very special year for Wilt Chamberlain. He scored 50 points or more in 46 games and became the first player in NBA history to score 4,000 points in a season. Chamberlain is a member of the Basketball Hall of Fame.

#4 ***Answer: Tyrone "Muggsy" Bogues*** of the Charlotte Hornets is 5 feet 3 inches tall, making him the shortest player in National Basketball Association history. On December 27, 1974, Muggsy became the 26th player to record 5,000 assists in an NBA career. He is ranked sixth on the career assist list among current NBA players.

Mugsy Bogues stands next to bent-over teammate Rafael Addison.

#5 ***Answer: In NBA games, each team is given 24 seconds to shoot the ball.*** If a team cannot shoot in 24 seconds, the other team gets the ball. In the early 1950s, there was no 24-second clock. Players could take as long as they wanted before shooting the ball. Back then, games were low scoring. If a team was winning, the players could just pass the ball around for as long as they wanted, keeping the other team away from the ball until the game was over. In 1953, Danny Biasone, owner of the Syracuse Nats, experimented with timing his players on offense during practice with a stopwatch. After discovering that the games were played faster, he recommended using a clock in official NBA games. On October 30, 1954, the first game with a 24-second clock was played. How did Danny Biasone come up with 24 seconds for his clock? Why not 30, 29, or 48 seconds? Biasone figured out that two teams took about 120 shots per game. He divided 120 into the length of a game, 48 minutes or 2,880 seconds, to come up with 24 seconds.

#6 ***Answer: Cheryl Miller.*** Her California high school team, Riverside Poly, won 132 out of the 136 games Miller played. In her college career, Miller scored 3,018 points and collected 1,534 rebounds. She averaged 23.6 points per game and 12.0 rebounds per game. While she played for the University of Southern California, her team won 112 games and lost only 10. Cheryl's brother, Reggie, plays for the NBA's Indiana Pacers. Cheryl Miller is a member of basketball's Hall of Fame.

Cheryl Miller

Ann Meyers

#7 ***Answer: Ann Meyers.*** In 1979 she signed a contract with the Indiana Pacers. Although her skills impressed the coaches, they felt she was too small to go up against the NBA's big men.

#8

Answer: Karl Malone. Malone is the only player in NBA history to score at least 2,000 points in nine seasons. He has a career scoring average of 26.1 points per game. Karl is called The Mailman because he always delivers. Instead of delivering mail, Karl delivers points.

Karl Malone

Anfernee Hardaway

#9

Answer: Anfernee Hardaway. When Anfernee was a boy, his grandmother called him "Pretty." Other people thought she was saying "Penny" instead, and began using that term for a nickname. Penny Hardaway still has the nickname he was given when he was growing up.

#10

Answer: The Boston Celtics won more games (2,437) and more championships (16) through 1996–97 than any other team in NBA history.

Resources to Check Out

Books

Anderson, Dave. *The Story of Basketball*. New York: Morrow, 1988.

Klinzing, Jim, and Mike Klinzing. *Fundamental Basketball*. Minneapolis: Lerner Publications, 1996.

Raber, Thomas R. *Michael Jordan: Basketball Skywalker*. Minneapolis: Lerner Publications, 1997.

Townsend, Brad. *Shaquille O'Neal: Center of Attention*, rev. ed. Minneapolis: Lerner Publications, 1998.

Wolf, Alexander. *One Hundred Years of Hoops*. New York: Time, Inc., 1991.

Web sites

http://www.nba.com
http://www.usabasketball.com

Photo credits

Photographs are reproduced with permission by: University Archives, University of Kansas, pp. 6, 13; Naismith Memorial Basketball Hall of Fame, pp. 7, 8, 24; Brown Brothers, pp. 11, 14, 17, 18 (left), 33, 35; UPI/Corbis-Bettmann, pp. 18 (right), 21 (left), 26, 59 (left and right); Andrew D. Bernstein/© NBA Photos, pp. 20, 60 (left); Independent Picture Service, pp. 21 (right), 28 (bottom left), 54 (left); Beloit College Archives, p. 22; Harlem Globetrotters International, Inc., p. 25; Dick Raphael/© NBA Photos, p. 27; John Biever, p. 28 (top left); Ken Regan/©NBA Photos, p. 28 (top right); Allen Einstein/© NBA Photos, p. 28 (bottom right); AP/Wide World Photos, p. 30 (left); Photography, Inc., p. 30 (right); Smith College Archives, p. 32; Archive Photos/Lambert, p. 37; Greg Shamus/© NBA Photos, p. 39; Reuters/John Kuntz/Archive Photos, p. 41; Nathaniel S. Butler/© NBA Photos, pp. 43, 47 (top left), 55 (bottom right); Sam Forencich/© NBA Photos, p. 45 (left); Bill Baptist/© NBA Photos, pp. 45 (right), 47 (bottom left), 57; Scott Cunningham/© NBA Photos, p. 47 (top right); John Greishop/© NBA Photos, pp. 47 (bottom right), 52 (bottom left); National Basketball Association, p. 49; Andy Hayt/© NBA Photos, p. 52 (top right); © NBA Photos, p. 53, 54 (right); Houston Rockets, p. 55 (top); Glenn James/© NBA Photos, p. 55 (bottom left); © ALLSPORT USA/Stephen Dunn, p. 58; Fernando Medina/© NBA Photos, p. 60 (right). Cover photo by Brown Brothers.

Bibliography

Ashe, Arthur Jr. *A Hard Road to Glory: the African American Athlete in Basketball.* New York: Amistad Press, 1988.

Bole, Robert D. and Alfred C. Lawrence. *From Peach Baskets to Slam Dunks: A Story of Professional Basketball.* Lebanon, NH: Whitman Press, 1987.

Bonavita, Mark, Mark Broussard, and Sean Stewart. *The Official NBA Register: 1995–1996.* St. Louis, MO: The Sporting News Publishing Co., 1995.

Bonavita, Mark, Mark Broussard, and Sean Stewart. *The Official NBA Register: 1996–1997.* St. Louis, MO: The Sporting News Publishing Co., 1996.

George, Nelson. *Elevating the Game: Black Men and Basketball.* New York: Harper-Collins, 1992.

Goldaper, Sam and Arthur Pincus. *How to talk Basketball.* New York: Dembner Books, 1983.

Hill, Bob and Randall Baron. *The Amazing Basketball Book: The First 100 Years.* Louisville, KY: Devyn Press, 1987.

Hollander, Zander, ed. *The NBA Book of Fantastic Facts, Feats, and Superstars.* New York: Rainbow Bridge Publishers, 1996.

Hull, Joan S. and Marianna Trekell, eds. *A Century of Women's Basketball: From Frailty to Final Four.* Reston, VA: American Alliance for Health, Physical Education, Recreation, & Dance, 1991.

Peterson, Robert W. *Cages to Jump Shots: Pro Basketball's Early Years.* New York: Oxford University Press, 1990.

The Official NBA Basketball Encyclopedia. Second edition. New York: Villard Press, 1994.

About the Author

Bruce Adelson is a sports writer, substitute teacher, and former attorney whose published works include *The Minor League Baseball Book*. His work has also appeared in *The Four Sport Stadium Guide* and in publications such as *The Washington Post, Sport Magazine,* and *Baseball America.* The Sports Trivia books are his first children's publications. Adelson lives in Alexandria, Virginia.

About the Illustrator

Harry Pulver Jr. is an illustrator and animator who also plays the accordian and guitar. His work has appeared in numerous national ad campaigns and in books, including *Find It!* and *Tracking the Facts,* two other titles by Lerner Publications.